THE
Greatest
POWER
THINKER
WHO EVER
LIVED

by Dr. Robert Schuller

*Dedicated to the memory
of my beloved friend
in Christ—*

NORMAN VINCENT PEALE

1898 - 1993

*He knew, and loved,
and embraced the faith of*
THE GREATEST
POWER THINKER
WHO EVER LIVED!

*Robert Schuller
January 1994*

Power Thinking...

Starts by rejecting Impossibility Thinking

You know what impossibility thinking is?

It's the kind of thinking that says:

> **"It's impossible!"**
> **"It won't work."**
> **"It'll never happen."**
> **"I haven't got what it takes."**
> **"Why bother to try?"**

So  ESUS

should have been the world's greatest
impossibility thinker,

For He had _nothing_ going for Him.

Positive Thinking...

It's **_Faith!_**
The birth of the belief that, "I *am* <u>somebody</u>!"
So, "I *can do* <u>something</u>."

Possibility Thinking...

It's *Faith* that is <u>Focused</u>!
"How can I possibly do it?"
See and seize the opportunity?
Shape and solve the problems?
Capture and sculpture the challenges?
Somehow—It's all Possible...
If I practice Power Thinking...

Power Thinking...

"It's <u>focused</u> *faith* that FOLLOWS THROUGH!
No stone left unturned.
No job left undone.
No possibility left undetected, undeveloped!
No price left unpaid!
No wonder **Positive Thinking**, **Possibility Thinking** and **Power Thinking** add up to sensational success!

You're ready to meet the greatest **Power Thinker** who ever lived.

ℐESUS was

a member of a despised minority,
a citizen of an occupied country,
a nobody as far as the Romans were
    concerned,
a joke to the occupying power,
a nuisance to His fellow Jews.

There was also an inscription over him, "This is the King of the Jews." (Luke 23:38)

4

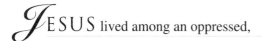

JESUS lived among an oppressed,

cynical and
embittered people!

Taxes were oppressive.
Freedom was unknown.
Survival was uncertain.
Religion was restrictive, negative, and joyless.

Yet Jesus never made an inflammatory speech,
never organized a guerrilla force, and
never led a march on Jerusalem or Rome.

*Now when he heard that John had been arrested, he
withdrew into Galilee. (Matthew 4:12)*

*J*ESUS inherited no illustrious name.

His father was a common laborer.
His mother was a simple, homespun type.
His uncles and aunts: who were they?
His grandparents? Nobody's!

He could never point with pride to a
prestigious address. Rather,
He came from a city reputed to be culturally
deprived and morally corrupt.
"Can anything good come out of Nazareth?"
was a common expression.

*"Is not this the carpenter's son?...Where then did
this man get all this?" (Matthew 13:55,56)*

*J*ESUS was uneducated.

Whatever His schooling was, it was simple.
The only account of His writing was a line
He scribbled in the sand.
He had

      no academic degrees,
      no certificates of special merit, award or
      achievement;
      no trophies or medals;
      And He never received an honorary
      doctorate of divinity degree!

*Jesus bent down and wrote with his finger on the
ground. (John 8:6)*

*J*ESUS lived and died untraveled.

He never visited the exciting, glamorous world out-
side His own country. He saw none of the sights so
important to the secular world of His day:

> The glistening temples of Athens;
> The Parthenon on the Acropolis holding the
> golden statue of Athena;
> Or Rome—with its impressive forum, colos-
> seum, and theaters;
> or—the marble, pillar-lined streets of
> Alexandria.
> Or the spectacular city of Ephesus!

All He saw were people: lonely, hurting, sick,
depressed, fearful, troubled hearts!
It made Him cry!

*And He went about all Galilee, teaching in their
synagogues and preaching the gospel of the kingdom and healing every disease and every infirmity
among the people. (Matthew 4:23)*

*J*ESUS never became an intimate friend

of men of power and influence.

> He had no "big connections,"
> V.I.P's did not seek Him out.
> Had He ever been asked for letters of
> character reference—whom could He list?
> No peer professors, famous authors,
> powerful politicians, ranking generals,
> or lordly churchmen.
>
> He couldn't have been a name-dropper
> if He wanted to! (Except to say—as He
> did—that He and God were very close.)

And as He was walking in the temple, the chief priests and the scribes and the elders came to him, and they said to him, "By what authority are you doing these things, or who gave you this authority to do them?" (Mark 11:27)

*J*ESUS had no organization.

> His followers were men with
> > broken speech,
> > rough hands and
> > cracked fingernails.

> They were
> > unpolished, uncultured, unlettered
> > and ignorant failures,

> In many ways, and in critical times, they
> proved to be
> > unstable,
> > uncertain,
> > undependable and
> > disappointing.

And he came to the disciples and found them sleeping, and he said, "...So, could you not watch with me one hour?"...leaving them again, he went away and prayed the third time...(Matthew 26:40,44)

Yes, *J*ESUS knew

> ingratitude,
> rejection,
> misunderstanding, and
> betrayal!

*J*ESUS—by all the psychological laws of

human development, should have lived and died a

> judgmental,
> frustrated,
> critical,
> angry,
> unbelieving,
> cynical,
> rebellious,
> violence-prone,
> emotionally-deprived,
> radically militant revolutionary!

Then all the disciples forsook Him and fled.
(Matthew 26:56)
Were not ten cleansed? (Luke 17:17)
Was no one found to return and give praise to God
except this foreigner? (Luke 17:18)

*J*ESUS lived and died in poverty. He had:

No home of His own,
No insurance policy,
No social security cards,
No retirement plan;
He performed a miracle to raise the money
to pay His taxes!

His estate? He left behind only His simple
robe, a cheap prize to entice the gambling
soldiers at the cross.

So He died empty-handed—except for fresh
  wounds—
Leaving no fortune and no heirs.

*And Jesus said to him, "Foxes have holes, and birds
of the air have nests; but the Son of man has
nowhere to lay his head." (Matthew 8:20)*

JESUS remained unmarried,

a single adult
all His life.

So He spent His years without the
encouragement
comfort or
companionship
of a wife or children.

In society where children were a man's
greatest treasure, He died
never having fathered
a single son or daughter.

So He died.
Childless.

*But He said to them, "I have food to eat of which
you do not know." (John 4:32)*

ESUS

Think of it: At His death
He was only thirty-three years old!
He was so young.
He died before His mother!
He was not given a half-century, or
more, to make His mark, write His
books, build His empire, and
conquer the world.

This—at least and at last—should have made
Him a
cynical impossibility thinker, crying out
through tight
lips, and bitter tears:

"It isn't fair!"
"I'm too young to die!"
"Others live long and longer—
why can't I?"
"Oh God—give me more time!"

ESUS

Where was His Heavenly Father
when Jesus needed Him most?

ESUS

All His life was good, kind and loving,
and very religious.
Every Sabbath—He was in the synagogue.
The Holy Scriptures—how He loved to read
them.
Prayer? His life was a prayer for all seasons!

ESUS

How He loved His Heavenly Father.
How He trusted His Heavenly Father.
How He served His Heavenly Father.

ESUS

Now on His cross—when He needs His God
   most—
God seems to have abandoned Him.

"My God, my God, why hast thou forsaken me?"
(Matthew 27:46)

15

ESUS

had every reason to be a negative
thinker. "I'm nobody, I can't do
anything."

ESUS

had every reason to be an
impossibility thinker. "I wish I
could but 'It's impossible'."

But, MIRACLE OF MIRACLES!

ESUS

Was a Positive, Possibility Thinker,
a Power Thinker!

This man Jesus turned out to be

THE WORLD'S GREATEST POWER THINKER!

No founder of any religion ever used the word **POSSIBLE** more than Jesus did!

> *"...for with God all things are POSSIBLE."*
> *(Mark 10:27)*

> *The things which are impossible with men are POSSIBLE with God. (Luke 18:27)*

> *All things are POSSIBLE to those who believe. (Mark 9:23)*

> *Father, all things are POSSIBLE...*
> *(Mark 14:36)*

> *If you have faith as a grain of mustard seed, you will say to this mountain, "Move..." and nothing will be impossible.*
> *(Matthew 17:20)*

> *"...with God nothing will be impossible."*
> *(Luke 1:37)*

> *With men it is impossible, but not with God."*
> *(Mark 10:27)*

> *"...but with God all things are POSSIBLE."*
> *(Matthew 19:26)*

ESUS

talked about His **POWER...**
Jesus encouraged others to tap into
His **POWER...**
and Jesus daily demonstrated His **POWER:**

> *"The Son of Man has **POWER** on earth to forgive sins." (Matthew 9:6)*

> *"Now when the multitudes saw it, they marveled and glorified God who had given such **POWER** to men." (Matthew 9:8)*

> *"And the **POWER** of the Lord was present to heal them." (Luke 5:17)*

> *"And the whole multitude sought to touch Him, for **POWER** went out from Him and healed them all." (Luke 6:19)*

> *"Behold, I send the promise of My Father upon you; but tarry in the city of Jerusalem until you are endued with **POWER** from on high." (Luke 24:49)*

> *"You shall receive **POWER** when the Holy Spirit has come upon you; and you shall be witnesses to the ends of the earth." (Acts 1:8)*

18

> *"And to those who overcome, and keep My words until the end, to these I will give* **POWER** *over the nations." (Revelation 2:26)*

And many of the witnesses to Jesus' glory wrote about His **POWER:**

> *"For I am not ashamed of the Gospel of Christ, for it is the* **POWER** *of God to salvation for everyone who believes." (Romans 1:16)*

> *"For the message of the cross is foolishness to those who are perishing, but to us who are being saved it is the* **POWER** *of God." (I Corinthians 1:18)*

> *"Finally, my brethren, be strong in the Lord and in the* **POWER** *of His might." (Ephesians 6:10)*

> *"For God has not given us a spirit of fear, but of* **POWER** *and of love and of a sound mind." (2 Timothy 1:7)*

> *"And His divine* **POWER** *has given to us all things that pertain to life and godliness, through the knowledge of Him who called us by glory and virtue." (2 Peter 1:3)*

19

To ESUS

Every problem was a possibility in disguise.

Sickness—was an opportunity for healing.
Sin—was an opportunity for forgiveness.
Sorrow—was an opportunity for
compassion.

Personal abuse was an opportunity to leave
a good impression and show the world how
possibility thinkers react!

*And He said to him, "Truly, I say to you, today you
will be with Me in Paradise." (Luke 23:43)*

To ESUS

Every person was a goldmine of
undiscovered hidden possibilities!

Peter? A tough-talking fisherman:
   But—he could make a great
   leader of a great new church.
Mary Magdalene? A common prostitute:
   But—she could become a sensitive,
   sweet soul. She could one day anoint
   His body for burial.
Matthew? A vulgar materialist:
   But—he had possibilities to become
   a great writer! Even the gospel!

No wonder Jesus rushed to meet the outcast,
riff-raff of humanity!

*And when Jesus came to the place, he looked up and
said to him, "Zacchaeus, make haste and come down;
for I must stay at your house today!
(Luke 19:5)*

To ESUS

The important fact about you and me
> is not that
> **WE ARE SINNERS**
> but that
> **WE CAN BECOME SAINTS.**

So Jesus never called any <u>person</u> a sinner!
He became angry only with religious people
who made people feel they were miserable,
guilty sinners.

Instead Jesus rushed to build—in the worst
of sinners—a belief that they, too, could be
saved for inspiring service!

"You are the salt of the earth..." (Matthew 5:13)
"You are the light of the world..." (v.14)
"Follow me and I will make you fishers of men."
(4:19)

22

So *J*ESUS proclaimed the most powerful

possibility:

The immeasurable

Mercy of God

He said to them, "Those who are well have no need of a physician, but those who are sick; I came not to call the righteous, but sinners." (Mark 2:17)

To ESUS

the whole world was
> **jammed,**
> **pregnant,**
> **loaded,**
> **bulging, with**
>> **untapped,**
>> **undiscovered,**
>> **undetected**

Potential!

That's
Power Thinking!

Then He said to His disciples, "The harvest is plentiful, but the laborers are few; pray therefore the Lord of the harvest to send out laborers into his harvest." (Matthew 9:37,38)

For God so loved the world that He gave His only Son that whoever believes in Him should have eternal life. (John 3:16)

*J*ESUS really believed in the

ultimate potential!

Jesus preached these grand possibilities:

>Man *can* be born again!
>Character *can* be changed!
>You *can* become a new person!
>Life *can* be beautiful!
>There *is* a solution to every problem!
>There *is* light behind every shadow!

...with God all things are possible. (Matthew 19:26)
...whoever believes in him should have eternal life.
(John 3:16)
Jesus answered him, "Truly, truly I say to you,
unless one is born anew, he cannot see the kingdom
of God. (John 3:3)

Yes, *JESUS* had an unshakable faith in these

ultimate possibilities:

> God exists!
> Life goes on beyond death!
> Heaven is for real!
>
> He has proven it:
> by dying—and rising again!

He saw the possibility of
> ultimate justice!
> So
> He had as much to say about hell
> as He did about heaven.

"O death where is your victory?
O death where is your sting?"
Thanks be to God, who gives us
the victory through our Lord Jesus Christ.
(I Corinthians 15:55,57)

*J*ESUS was the great empowerer;

He saw the reality of heaven and hell in eternity.
He also saw the possibility of a transformed
world—
here on planet earth.
He was impressed by what the world could
become—
never depressed by what the world was.
He truly believed in the possibility of
transformed lives.
He truly believed that common people can
become—
uncommonly powerful.
He knew without a shadow of doubt that
ordinary persons
could become extraordinary persons if they
could—
become POWER THINKERS.

So He would give self-confidence to
inferiority-complexed people.
He would make it possible for guilt-infected,
failure-plagued, problem-swamped persons
to start loving themselves and stop hating
themselves!

*"Go into all the world and preach the gospel to the
whole creation." (Mark 16:15)*

ESUS

What enormous self-confidence this
unmatched Power Thinker had! Listen
to what Christ said:

> *"I am the good shepherd." (John 10:11)*

> *"I am the door; if any one enters by me,
> he will be saved..." (John 10:9)*

> *"I am the bread of life..." (John 6:35)*

> *"I am the vine, you are the branches,
> He who abides in me, and I in him,
> he it is that bears much fruit..." (John 15:5)*

"I am the way, and the truth, and the life; no one comes to the Father, but by me." (John 14:6)

"I am the resurrection and the life; he who believes in me, though he die, yet shall he live..." (John 11:25)

Then came the end. He was accused
of stirring up the people.

He was placed on trial.

He was charged with blasphemy—did
He not claim to be the promised
Messiah?

At least, did He not allow people to
get the impression that He was the
Son of God?

In His public trial He was
challenged to deny His deity, to
withdraw His blasphemous statements,
and clear up the confused minds of
the simple people who believed Him
to be God visiting earth in human
form.

But He could not tell a lie, so He
remained silent.

The verdict was predictable: death
by crucifixion!

A crowd gathered to see how a
possibility thinker dies.

How did He die?

He died seeing and seizing the
possibilities of the moment!

He practiced what He had preached
all His life!

He turned the hell into a heaven.

"...today you will be with me in Paradise."
(Luke 23:43)

Here was His chance to teach the world how
forgiving God can be!

*"Father, forgive them; for they know not what they
do." (Luke 23:34)*

31

This was a spectacular opportunity to dramatically teach all men of all ages to come, that death can be a grand reunion with God!

So His last spoken words were loaded with great expectations. "Father, into Your hands I commit my spirit." (Luke 23:46)

There was a final gasp—and He was gone. The Roman commander in charge of the execution turned away—converted on the spot, he was overheard saying, "Certainly this man was innocent!" (Luke 23:47)

His body was taken down and sealed in a tomb. Then it happened! Easter morning dawned! He was resurrected! He came back to life again.

Why do we believe this fantastic tale? Because of the incredible change in His followers. They saw Him alive again.

Where they were cowards, they became fearless proclaimers in the city streets—in daylight!

Where they were impossibility thinkers —they became possibility thinkers!

Where they were weak thinkers–they became POWER THINKERS!

**THINK DEEPLY, PASSIONATELY
ABOUT YOUR PERSONAL
      POTENTIAL!
YOUR UNTAPPED POSSIBILITIES,
YOUR EMERGING EMPOWERMENT!**

For, today, twenty centuries later, Christ literally
lives in millions of human beings all around
the world!

By His death He solved His greatest
problem. What was that?

He could only be in one place at a time. Now,
through the power of His Holy Spirit, He is able to
live in millions of lives. all around the world! Think
of the possibilities:

> Christ can infiltrate
>> any race,
>> any religion,
>> any community,
>> any country,
>> any culture!

The Good News is—
Christ Can Live in You!

ESUS

That is what authentic Christianity is all about!

BEING A CHRISTIAN IS
offering yourself to Him

Your mind—for Christ to think through,
Your heart—for Christ to love through,
Your lips—for Christ to speak through,
Your hands—for Christ to touch through!!

Just imagine what possibilities for exciting living
this opens up to you!

*It is no longer I who lives but Christ who lives in
me. (Galatians 2:20)*

If Christ can live within you then it is possible for you, too,

> To—Live an empowered life!
> To—Turn your problems into opportunities!
> To—Tackle your opportunities and succeed!
> To—Dream great dreams and make them come true!
> To—Switch from jealousy and self-pity to really caring about others who are much worse off than you are.
> To—Pick up the broken hopes and start over again!
> To—See great possibilities in those unattractive people!
> To—Become a truly beautifully person— like Jesus!

I can do all things in him who strengthens me. (Philippians 4:13)

Your Prayer for a New and Exciting Life

Jesus Christ—I've come to see that many things are possible that I never before believed were possible.

I believe it's possible—that You were sent by God into the world to be my Savior. I accept You now.

I believe it's possible—eternal life!

I believe it's possible—that Christ is alive this moment and trying to penetrate my life through my brain as I read these words!

I believe it's possible—for His Holy Spirit to live within me! I confess my sin.
I ask Christ to save me.
I invite Him to come into my life.
I believe it's possible!

Lord, I invite you to come and live your life in my life today.

Lord, here is my brain—think with it.

Lord, here is my face—smile through it.

Lord, here is my tongue—so speak to people with it.

Lord, here is my ear—listen to persons with it.

Lord, here is my hand—touch someone with it.

Lord, here are my arms—lift and hug someone with them.

Lord, here are my feet—walk with them where you want to go today.

Lord, I want to be a beautiful "Christ—In Person."

Amen

Now pray this Possibility-Thinking prayer every day:

> **Lord, show me the person**
> **You want to speak to**
> **through my life today.**

Amen.